Stereotypical Perceptions
Redefining How We Think

Joann Watts-Sietas, Ph.D.

Printed in the United States of America

FOCUS PUBLICATIONS®
FOLSOM, U. S. A.

Table of Contents

FOREWORD

"Judging a person does not define who they are,

it defines who you are."

The book *Stereotypical Perceptions: Redefining How We Think* written by Joann Watts-Sietas, Ph.D gives the reader(s) a very deep, educational and passionate reflection in understanding stereotypical perceptions in American society. She also gives an historical overview from the very beginning of this country until present times. The author is able to show some of the reasons behind these perceptions, as well as the many forms, which are based on her own personal and professional experience. Growing up as a little girl in Louisiana positions the author to speak candidly about her experience. Moreover, even as an adult, she continues to observe or encounter these perceptions almost on a regular basis in society. Despite a lifetime of negative experiences, this did not make her bitter or angry. This, in turn, made her curious and eager to take a more critical and analytical look at society. These encounters prompted her interest and passion to educate others and provide them with new knowledge and information regarding stereotypical perceptions.

Dr. Sietas has never stopped learning and experiencing new things in her life, which has expanded her knowledge and given her the ability to give back to others. One of her ways to gain more knowledge and experiences in her life is one of her greatest passions: traveling. Dr. Sietas has traveled to almost every continent and spent valuable time in many countries with different cultures and people. In doing so, she has realized the many benefits of stepping out of her own cultural circle and country to face a new frontier and different ways of living. She believes that we do gain so much by immersing ourselves in new cultures. As such, we become more understanding and tolerant of different people and better connected to the lives they live. In addition, we learn valuable skills that we can take back home.

Dr. Sietas believes that the ability to look beneath the surface to discern the human strengths and weaknesses of people different from ourselves is the beginning of a journey of self and human discovery upon which our own human fulfillment depends. Further, the advantage of cultural diversity and sensitivity presents the individual with larger possibilities of life in an inherently diverse world through exposure to other people and their ways. Cultural diversity is important to her and is an essential trait which guides her understanding of the world. Hence, as a society, she also believes that we must move away from an inherited context of assumptions and generalizations about others to thinking more critically. As a resourceful and positive thinking individual, I have seen what can be accomplished with her vision, followed by hard work, creative solutions, personal introspection, mentoring and partnership. If you decide to read her book, it is my hope that it inspires you to reach out to others that are different from you. If you decide to give this book to someone else, it is my hope that the words in this book will float like the seeds of tulips, landing softly where they need to be.

- Ingo Sietas
California 2020

PREFACE

Race and ethnic relations discourse is a challenging and dynamic field of study. The United States is a multicultural nation comprised of indigenous peoples and others who themselves or whose ancestors once lived in another nation. The population represents different nationalities, social classes, religions, and native languages. Each group in our society is part of a larger process where behavioral patterns are inherited contexts from past generations. Cohorts are bound together by similar circumstances, and, needless to say, as a country, many take pride in being a nation of immigrants. Many people around the world view the United States as the land of opportunity whereby people can improve their lives. There are countless testimonies that support this ideal. However, there are many who testify to the contrary. There is a disquieting truth that contradicts the evidence of freedom of choice, economic opportunity and upward mobility.

The American Dream has become a nightmare for many who continue to struggle but are unable to get ahead. The treatment of Black Americans illustrates the continued persistence of suppressive and entrenched inequality and racism. Today's ethnic tension and hatred dates back to the beginning of slavery. When the colonizers arrived on the continent of Africa, they did not know what to make of their encounters with Africans. This was the beginning of racializing.

Currently, political rhetoric and systemic racism are entwined, and this continues to propagate racist ideology. It is a truism that the notions of prejudice and hostility have their basis in ignorance, as much as is the ideal that social intimacy with Black Americans and other people of color implies acceptance and equality.

The future of our nation is at a crossroad and it is imperative that we talk effectively with one another and reach a mutual understanding that we are all human beings. The inability to view Black Americans in terms of their achievements and contributions to society is usually symptomatic of a systemic lack of cultural sensitivity towards other groups and lack of education about diversity. As a result, this lack of reflection and understanding engenders negative social dispositions, including feelings of hostility and bigotry toward Black Americans and other people of color. The opposite of this mindset is the ability to alter one's perception, which is the hallmark of a balanced unbiased outlook.

The consequences of prejudicial attitudes undermine our national unity. The "racial problem" often distracts people in society from seeing realistic solutions for other pressing social and economic problems that face many people of color. Intolerance of each other leads to fear and uneasiness among members of the privileged majority, as well as its victims. Hatred of others fails to make the maladjusted person feel more secure and socially adapted. Further prejudicial attitudes not only severely limit the opportunities for people of color, they also make it more difficult to develop an integrated and well-adjusted personality. In addition, prejudicial attitudes deprive certain people in society momentarily or for the rest of their lives of dialogue and mental development. Social psychologist Triandis has pointed out that stereotyping is a natural phenomenon in that all humans develop mental categories to help make sense of their environment. We stereotype because it is impossible for the human brain to employ all the information present in man's environment. Further, there is a natural tendency to simplify our problems and to solve them as easily as possible. A "pet formula," such as "Black Americans are not smart," makes it possible for an Anglo employer to eliminate much of his mental effort by simply not considering Black Americans for jobs in his firm. If he were to check on each applicant and to understand the causes of his behavior, he would have to work much harder. Moreover, categorization helps perceptions. For example, we are told to be careful and constantly to watch out for "drunk drivers." Upon doing so, our driving instantly becomes more defensive. The category "drunk" implies many behaviors on the part of the other driver, and we adjust to them quickly and usefully. But categorization also has a penalty. The broader the categories, the more inaccurate they are likely to be. The more they help us to simplify our problems, the more likely they are to cause us to perceive the world incorrectly.

This book deals with the formation of stereotypes, how to eradicate these constructs about racial and ethnic groups, how the film and media industry has propagated pervasive images of Black Americans dating back as far as colonization of America, and the illusion of fairness in the criminal justice system. It is my hope that this book stimulates critical thinking and dialogue about stereotypes, racism and social justice in America, engages readers on an emotional level, and moves them to self-reflection. We must remember that no child is born prejudiced. Prejudices are learned within a context influenced by personal needs and social influence.

INTRODUCTION

See that man over there?

Yes.

Well, I hate him.

But you don't know him.

That's why I hate him.

(Allport)

Many, but not all Americans, have forgotten that the Native Americans or first nation people lived on the North American continent for centuries before the Europeans arrived. To fully understand the dynamics of intergroup relations both in the past and the present, we must acknowledge another disquieting truth. Americans have not always welcomed newcomers with open arms. Indeed, they have often responded with overt acts of prejudice and discrimination. The dominant group's treatment of Black Americans and Native Americans disturbingly illustrates the persistence of entrenched inequality and racism. Many members of each ethnic or racial group came to the "New World" for economic, political, or religious reasons, or sometimes for the adventure of beginning a new life in a new land. Conversely, there were others who were forced to immigrate. Picture yourself being imprisoned, chained and dragged out of your home and country to live in an unhappy exile and life of subservience. Most Africans arrived in America between 1619 and the end of the Atlantic slave trade in 1808. They left a world that had meaning, and whose beauty was now destroyed. The new society that they found themselves in was treacherous and valueless.

It is still a society of rich and poor, powerful and powerless. But the new rulers seem to have no traditions to restrain themselves, as neither custom nor religion limits their actions. This is the frame of mind that one has to appreciate in order to understand ideological dominance. According to conservative thought, stability, tradition, and order in social institutions, and not individual rights, are the basis of a "good society." However, this type of ideology implies the consent of subordinate groups to their own subordination. Ideological dominance among ruling elites seeks to perpetuate their own philosophy, culture, and morality, and render them unchallengeable and as part of the natural order of things. Today, these unchallenged structural strains are deep and solid. In order to disrupt the roots of this ideology, we must eradicate America's nationalism and conceptual

3

framework that make others believe that the United States of America is the only desirable place to live in the world.

Being born and raised in this country, I am not convinced that this is a "great nation." The elements of a great nation are measured by the way people are treated. What is denied must be recognized! Life, liberty and the pursuit of happiness are incongruent with the pathological behavior evidenced by America's history. While we cannot change our ignoble past, we can, at least, not be indifferent to the contemporary suffering that is linked to that past. For example, it is morally and intellectually superficial to begin and end one's argument with the observation that the problems of the underclass are due to their high rates of criminal behavior and out of wedlock births, and not to racism and prejudice. But this is what the discourse assessing the status of Black Americans and other people of color has come to. In order to have an honest conversation about racism and prejudicial attitudes, we must include in our political and academic discourse the contributions of slavery. This would allow students to acquire a deeper understanding of how racism formed in the United States as a structural phenomenon, touching people's everyday lives. Many of us are still very parochial, having little or no experience of individuals from backgrounds different from our own. As a society, we continue to depend on stereotypes, which are mostly negative generalizations about racial and ethnic groups that emerge from social curricula. The social distance of Blacks from Whites is such a marked feature of race relations in the United States that, indeed, only a small minority of Whites could rightfully claim that "some of their best friends" are black. No people of color wear the protective bubble of "white privilege," and this bubble is something that all those with darker skins are weary of trying to get people not of color to understand. Many of my "white" colleagues have often stated, "We must own it," meaning they should not deny the historical and present benefits of being white in America.

As an educator, you are expected to build critical thinking skills in students, which includes posing challenging questions to them and teaching the value of comparing and contrasting, as everything is not simply either right or wrong. In essence, the challenge for many educators is to move students beyond personal opinions or life experiences by prompting them to research the existing body of knowledge, which would allow a reflective and reasonable thought process.

During my twenty plus years of teaching theoretical concepts, which has been in predominantly "white conservative communities," many students, as well as the educational institutions, have not been prepared for such dialogue. Due to the under representation of black professors, staff and students have had limited to no interaction with black authority figures in the classroom. This alone has made it difficult for students to be engaging and participatory in collaborative discussions about systemic racism and ethnic relations in America. The lack of diversity witnessed throughout community colleges and universities hurts both individual students and the working environment. It has generated tensions that distort cultural understanding and narrow the educational experiences of many students. The majority of my students were educated in overwhelmingly predominate "white" conservative schools with little or no contact with people of color, specifically, Black Americans and Latino professors. Moreover, having their first exposure to a classroom with a professor/ educator of color, students generally will experience a different environment comparative to what they are familiar with. This rarity of interracial contact, combined with the prevailing conservative and white racial attitudes, thus underscores the validity of Allport's parable.

There is a new emergence of in-your-face systemic racism in this country. We are living in a time whereby non people of color, Whites, specifically, are calling 911 to a scene based on a community member's bias. Moreover, police officers should not include these biases in their policing. The worst case scenario is that law enforcement will show up with guns. Even in the best case scenario, Blacks will probably have to deal with the trauma of having been placed in mortal fear. But most of the time, there are no consequences for the people who weaponize their fear and use law enforcement as an extension of their "white privilege" and stereotypical perceptions of Black Americans. These experiences consist of short-term encounters whereby the individual is directly targeted. Still in the realm of racist thinking, as opposed to action, is racial or ethnic prejudice. It can take the form of beliefs about a group, negative feelings towards a group, or the desire to discriminate against a group. If I automatically don't like you because you are black, or if I want to discriminate against you because you are black, or if I think you are greedy because you are Jewish, I am prejudiced because I am responding to you entirely on the basis of your race or ethnicity. Moreover, I am choosing to ignore or disbelieve the influence of everything else about you, except the fact that you are black, Latino or Jewish. The most common form of prejudice is stereotypes which are constructed beliefs that all members of the same ethnic and racial group share given characteristics. These attributed characteristics are usually negative. These concrete and specific encounters are building blocks of experiences of being a target of prejudice and towards targets' general knowledge about prejudice. Since the experience of everyday prejudice is ongoing, the stigmatized individual or groups are able to anticipate prejudicial situations and develop strategies for dealing with these situations, which is a form of racial literacy.

It is important to note that individuals and groups are not passive victims who are unable to deflect the negative consequences of encountering prejudice, but are active agents who make choices in their lives about when to challenge or confront prejudice. This is played out today by the Black Lives Matter movement. The ongoing fatigue and frustration of dealing with prejudice takes a toll on the individual, as well as group members. Many years ago, but nonetheless relevant today, one of the nation's most talented journalists, Leanita McClain, committed suicide. She was the first Black American to serve on the Chicago Tribune's editorial board. Part of the investigation of McClain's suicide was an investigation into the pressures on black professionals in white America. In what she called a "generic suicide note," McClain herself suggested the complexity of the forces pushing her toward self-destruction. Writing in her careful Palmer-method longhand, she said, "Happiness is a private club that will not let me enter....Please let me go the way I choose. Do not try to pull me back into this world. I will never live long enough to see my people free anyway."

Many Blacks have undertaken the long journey from childhood poverty in socio economically deprived neighborhoods to jobs in white-dominated professions. Many of these racial pioneers may possess special reservoirs of eloquence, as did McClain. But they must withstand strains of isolation that Whites seldom encounter in achieving similar success. Black Americans not only face blatant prejudice and discrimination, but also suffer greatly from the subtle pressures to adapt to the values and ways of an overwhelmingly white environment. They often learn to wear a mask. Proactive coping skills are utilized frequently, and this includes the anticipation of stressful events and preparations to prevent or mute the effects of the stressor. In the case of prejudice targets, they can also use their knowledge of racial literacy and awareness of when, where, by whom and in what manner prejudice is most likely to occur. The anticipation of prejudice, however, may affect people's choices about how to present themselves, where to socialize, and where to live, go to college and work. The struggle of balancing a "double consciousness" creates a peculiar tension, as mentioned, which extracts the definition of one's true self from the treatment afforded the denigrated categories in which Black Americans are placed.

The checkerboard of prejudice in the United States of America is perhaps the most intricate of all. While some of the endless antagonism seems to be based upon realistic conflict of interest, most of it, we suspect, is a product of a lack of education about racial and ethnic groups, coupled with fear and hatred. The black color is a badge of inferiority that was devised to rationalize the exploitation of my ancestors (black slaves). There is a tragic irony here that a people who have been in America as long as the first white settlers should find themselves in a subordinate position today — a fact of American life.

Chapter 1

Stereotypes: An oversimplified image

Stereotypes are not the product of individual cognitive activity alone, but are also social and collective products which function ideologically by justifying and legitimizing existing social and power relations within a society. It is suggested, however, that individually held stereotypes are held by meaningful subgroups of the population who share perspectives based upon a common correlated variable. The social judgement literature has been criticized for its focus on errors made, which rarely involve social interaction of any kind. Researchers emphasize that social judgement occurs in a social context with contextual factors which can produce violations of logical principles when based upon prescriptive and rational theory. They further assert that contact does not only refer to the task situation or environment but also to the decision maker as an individual with a history of experience, prior learning and biological limitations. Therefore, the individual is part of the context of social judgement. Equally important is perhaps the most comprehensive model of social judgment application by Smith and Zarate, which emphasized the importance of the context and individual differences in perceivers' goals, past experiences and exposure to the larger group. The authors' overall thesis is that cognitive structures relating to a person's perception are exemplar-based, and that the exemplar drawn upon in any given judgement will depend on all of the above factors. They make a case for the overwhelming saliency of race in social judgement. For example, perceivers who are more racially prejudiced within the context of social judgement tend to pay more attention to a target's race, rather than to his or her occupation, personal characteristics or other attributes. More attention to race, in turn, means that all Blacks are perceived as relatively similar to each other and different from non-Blacks. Consider the salience and obviousness of cues for social categories like race, gender, and age, compared with less perceptually obvious categories like occupation or sexual orientation. In most everyday encounters in which the perceiver is not motivated to gather extensive additional information about the target, easily perceptible surface features will likely receive the bulk of the perceiver's attention. However, ease of perception is not the whole story for social and cultural factors to shape the meaning attached to attributes. The exemplar-based model states that perceiver contextual and motivational factors influence exemplar similarity. Further perceiver factors, such as motivation and prejudice, will cause individuals to store an attitude or motive consistent with the interpretation of the target group member, thus increasing the predominance of these features in the exemplars drawn upon in future interactions. Although salient features like race are most easily perceived, their model points to the insufficiency of this fact alone in explaining certain stereotype effects, as they recognize that "social and cultural factors shape the meaning attached to attributes like skin color" (Smith & Zárate, 1992, p 12). Moreover, the authors discuss how exposure and past experiences, as well as attitudes, affect judgments. In terms of exposure and past experiences, they point to the prevalence of particular associations between attributes and social roles. When group members are unequally distributed into particular social roles or economic statuses, the roles most associated with the group membership serve to increase the saliency and attention given to group membership and the corresponding attributes based on roles, even if out of context. An example of this scenario is the unequal distribution of women and men in the role of caregiver. Exposure studies assert that people who are usually exposed at a distance without involvement or intimacy will increase the number of stored exemplars with consistent stereotypical attributes. In contrast, increased familiarity with a group member resulting from extensive personal interaction over time, would expose the perceiver to counter stereotypic attributes, and a different type of stored exemplar would result. In addition, it is concluded that the importance of these knowledge structures varies, based upon all the context and individual differences. However, this group-level knowledge structure is important to the extent that it often does come into play. In view of these contributions, it seems likely that group stereotypic knowledge structures have substantial impact on perceptions of individuals belonging to salient identity groups, related to the content and accuracy of held stereotypes.

For the purpose of our discussion, "attitudes" are thought to refer to one's feelings about the target group, and "stereotypes" refer to generalized perceptions or beliefs about the attributes of the target group. Further adding to the negativity are theoretical assertions that stereotypes serve to help prejudiced individuals rationalize the personal biases they possess. Therefore, research aimed at determining the relative accuracy of such knowledge structures and who may be more or less accurate is important. Moreover, many factors may affect the content of individuals' stereotypes.

Chapter 2

Unconscious bias:
We live in society and society lives in us

There is widespread consensus that stereotypes are cognitive schemas, which is a concept or mental framework that helps organize and interpret information. They can be useful because they allow us to take shortcuts in interpreting the vast amount of information that is available in our environment. However, these mental frameworks also cause us to exclude pertinent information and to focus instead only on things that confirm our pre-existing beliefs and ideas. Prejudice is one example of a schema that prevents people from seeing the world as it is and inhibits them from taking in new information. Sometimes, it is easy to consider words and concepts as harmless abstractions. However, a moment's reflection on Western history gives the lie to this naive view. People's situations and social experiences influence their attitudes and beliefs. The principles of social psychology include affect, behavior, and cognition when applied to the study of stereotypes. The cognitive component is the most common form of prejudice (racial biases). According to Dr. Jennifer Eberhardt, "We stereotype because we are human and we cannot process data well. It's simply easier to put things and people into types and generalities than it is to process everything separately. And guess what, a lot of times we are right. But this is what lulls us into complacency and makes us think our stereotypes are reliable but they are not. They are misleading, dangerous and destructive, and can lead us into biases" (Starr, 2020). We live in society and society lives inside of us.

Eberhardt makes it clear that these biases tend to seep into aspects of our lives without our awareness. Her stance is made clear in her original research and relays that of others as well. For example, researchers Max Weisbuch, Kristin Panker, and Nalini Ambady chose eleven popular television shows that have positive representations of black characters, including *CSI* and *Grey's Anatomy,* where black characters are doctors, police officers, and scientists. The researchers showed study participants ten-second clips of a variety of white characters interacting with the same black characters, but with the sound muted and the black characters edited out of the frame. Participants who were unfamiliar with the shows were asked to watch a number of these clips and to rate how much each unseen character was liked and was being treated positively by the white characters on the screen.

Sometimes the unseen characters were black, and sometimes the unseen characters were white. A consistent pattern emerged when the researchers pooled the ratings: Participants perceived the unseen black characters in these popular shows to be less and treated less positively by the other characters than the unseen white characters. The black characters were surrounded by a cast of white characters, who, through their subtle facial expressions and body movements, communicated less regard for them. And the television viewers were affected by this: The more negative the nonverbal actions directed at the unseen black characters, the more anti black bias the study participants revealed in an implicit association test following the showing. That is, there was evidence for a type of "bias contagion." The researchers found this to be the case even though the study participants were unable to identify any consistent pattern in the treatment of white and black characters when asked to do so directly. Accordingly, it would seem that exposure and discussion in the right context can cure some bias. But this does not ensure that bias will eventually go away. We may decide that Italian Americans control organized crime, or that Black Americans are lazy. And we may use these beliefs to guide our actions toward people from these groups.

In addition to our stereotypes, we may develop prejudice, an unjustifiable negative attitude toward an out group or toward the members of that out group. Prejudice can take the form of dislike, anger, fear, disgust, discomfort and even hatred. These attitudes are often translated into fear of walking in the neighborhood of the out group, fear of being mugged by members of the out group, distrust of any merchant from the out group, fear of a member of the out group moving next door, and anger at any advantages that members of the out group may be perceived as benefiting from. People are prejudiced because they grew up in a prejudiced environment where they learn from significant others. The learning occurs throughout the processes of selective exposure, modeling, reward and punishment, and identification. If a person is exposed only to prejudiced attitudes and beliefs, they seem like unquestioned truths. The question remains: What about counter indoctrination? If the people you love and respect hold prejudiced beliefs, could such beliefs really be wrong? Researchers have shown that those whose parents and other childhood significant others were prejudiced tend themselves to be more prejudiced as adults. However, people can confirm to having no prejudice, as well as to having prejudice.

During the socialization process, individuals acquire the values, attitudes, beliefs, and perceptions of their culture. Generally, the child conforms to the parents' expectations in acquiring an understanding of the world and its people. Being impressionable and knowing no alternative conceptions of the world, the child usually accepts these concepts without questioning their parents.

Despite being based on stereotypes, prejudices shape our perception of various people, and this, in turn, influences our attitudes and actions toward out groups. For example, if we develop negative attitudes about Jews based on being taught that they are shrewd, acquisitive, and clannish, as adults, we may refrain from business or social relationships with them. We may not even realize the reason for such avoidance, so subtly has it been instilled within us.

In contrast, the theory of personality needs examines prejudice, arising largely from the work of Adorno and his colleagues. In their content analysis of speeches written by right-wing extremists, Adorno uncovered a number of themes not logically related but that nonetheless appeared repeatedly. He discovered that having a certain personality type he called the authoritarian personality does appear to be associated with prejudice. According to Adorno, highly prejudiced people are insecure conformists. They believe that things are either right or wrong. Ambiguity disturbs them, and they become anxious when they confront norms and values that are different from their own. After their analysis, Adorno and his colleagues developed a personality measure to rate distinct attitudes and beliefs, for example, excessive respect for authority, aggression against nonconformists, cynicism, and opposition to looking inward to understand oneself. This prejudiced individual meets two kinds of personality needs, which are scapegoating and projection. Scapegoating is when the prejudiced individual displaces feelings of anger or frustration that cannot be expressed toward the true source of the individual's feelings. Instead, they take out their frustrations on ethnic or religious minorities, or other groups who display nonconformity in their dress style. There are certain characteristics necessary for a group to become a suitable scapegoat. First, the group must be highly visible in physical appearance or observable customs and actions. Second, it must be not strong enough to strike back. Third, it must be situated with easy access of the dominant group and ideally concentrated in one area. Fourth, it must be a past target of hostility for whom latent hostility still exists.

The second personality need is called projection — a process by which a person denies or minimizes personal shortcomings by exaggerating the extent to which these same shortcomings occur in others. In particular, this person tends to exaggerate the faults of minority groups.

Research has consistently demonstrated that when members of a dominant group practice violence against a minority group and exploit it sexually, they are likely to believe that the minority group itself displays traits of sexual violence. Conversely, in apartheid South Africa, black males were thought to be sexually dangerous to white women — but, in fact, virtually all criminal sexual contact was initiated by white men against black women. Prejudicial stereotypes have a pervasive and often pernicious influence on our response to others, and also, in some cases, on our own behaviors. Let us turn to one particularly disturbing line of cognitive schemas research about the influence of prejudice on behaviors.

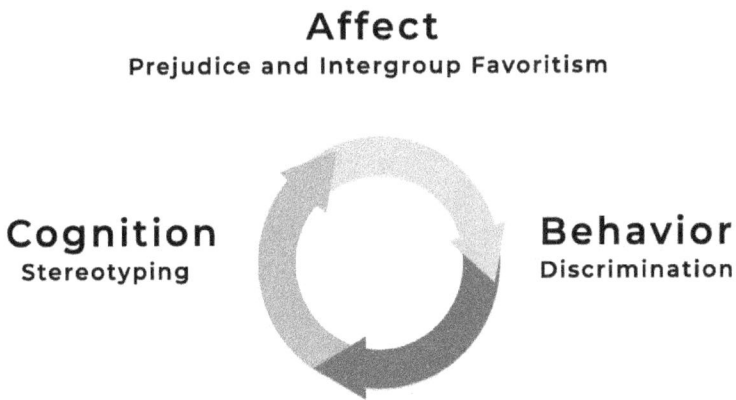

Affect
Prejudice and Intergroup Favoritism

Cognition
Stereotyping

Behavior
Discrimination

Figure 1. ABC- Affect Behavior Cognition

Professor Joshua Correll and his colleagues had white participants participate in an experiment in which they viewed photographs of white and black people on a computer screen. Across the experiment, the photographs showed the people holding either a gun or something harmless such as a cell phone. The participants were asked to decide as quickly as possible to press a button to "shoot" if the target held a weapon but to "not shoot" if the person did not hold a weapon. Overall, the white participants tended to shoot more often when the person holding the object was black, and this occurred even when there was no weapon present. Relationships among social groups are influenced by the ABCs of social psychology.

This experiment can be applied to the encounters that many Black American males have had with local law enforcement officers. The cognitive perception by the officers of black males often leads to disproportionately more Blacks being killed than Whites. This supports the movement Black Lives Matter. There was a shocking police shooting of a black man in July 2020 in Florida, whereby an unarmed black man with autism had wandered off and subsequently encountered a law enforcement officer. The man was told by the officer to lie on the ground and put his hands up in the air. Needless to say, he complied with the officer's directive, but the officer fired anyway, wounding him in the leg. The man asked the officer, "Why did you shoot me?" The officer replied, "I don't know." This incident fully supports Dr. Eberhardt's research to explore the insidious nature of unconscious bias, so that we are all more able to recognize instances of it in our thoughts, impulses and reactions. The extent to which that bias remains somewhat benign, or instead spreads into an active bias against another cohort, is more often a product of the prevailing norms and cultures in which we are raised.

It is natural to like some people and dislike others. However, we should not let a person's skin color, gender, age, religion, sexual orientation, or ethnic background make these determinations for us. And yet, despite our best intentions, we may end up making friends only with people who are similar to us or perhaps even avoiding people who we see as different.

The distinction between affect and cognition has been an essential one in understanding racial bias in inter-group relations. Dual processing theories inform us that people tend to use existing stereotypical knowledge rather than individuating information while communicating with a member of another cultural group. Research demonstrates that cognition-based stereotypes are better predictors of participants' social judgement and policy opinions, and that affect-based prejudice is a better predictor of social distance and non-verbal communication. Cognitive approaches to stereotyping do not adequately account for interracial encounters in particular. However, these encounters fail to address critical issues regarding intention, motivation and behavior. Cognitive approaches to stereotyping have, until recently, neglected such motivational factors in their rush to show normalization of stereotypes. Adding to the complexity of this concept is the fact that there are two quite different senses of stereotypes: cultural and individual. Cultural stereotypes are a set of shared beliefs held by an individual about a target group. Stereotypes, however, may involve affective reactions, as well as cognitive representations: that is, when stereotypes are activated, both cognitive and affective information becomes accessible.

Although theorists suggest that while stereotyping knowledge structures are real, they may come into play in some contexts, contingent upon the perceiver's history and motivation. Moreover, in view of these contributions, it seems likely that group stereotypic knowledge structures have substantial impact on perceptions of individuals belonging to salient identity groups. Recent research shows that stereotypes among Whites are important causes of discrimination against Black Americans in employment. Retrospectively, many researchers believe that modern prejudice has taken on a subtle form of symbolic racism. This term refers to a pattern in which people do not overtly express prejudice or racist ideas, but oppose social policies that would reduce inequality, such as reparation programs (affirmative action) and government spending to assist minorities. However, a substantial change has occurred in these attitudes over the past years, according to the National Opinion Research Center. Why are people opposed to such policies? Perhaps it is the perceived contention that the system is fair, that there is equal opportunity, and that minorities are mainly at fault for the disadvantages they suffer. Imagine this scenario: Mr. Bigot sees a well-dressed, white Anglo-Saxon sitting on a park bench sunning himself at three o'clock on a Wednesday afternoon and thinks nothing of it. If Mr. Bigot sees a well-dressed black man doing the same thing, he is liable to leap to the conclusion that the person is unemployed and he becomes infuriated because he assumes that his hard-earned taxes are paying that shiftless good-for-nothing enough in government subsides to keep him in good clothes. If Mr. Bigot passes Mr. Anglo's house and notices that a trash can is overturned and some garbage is strewn about, he is apt to conclude that a stray dog has been searching for food. If he passes Mr. Garcia's house and notices the same thing, he is inclined to become annoyed and assert that "Those people live like pigs." Not only does prejudice influence his erroneous conclusions, but it also justifies and intensifies his negative feelings.

The cultural screen that we develop and through which we view the world is not always accurate. But it does permit the transmission of shared values and attitudes which are reinforced by others. Learned prejudice is part of the socialization process. It is safe to conclude that prejudiced people see the world in an obscured way, and this reality continues to intensify.

Chapter 3
The illusion of fairness

Many governments have been founded upon the principle of the subordination of certain racial and ethnic groups. For much of our history, those who fought to free America from racial bigotry were animated by a common idea. They saw racism as a glitch, a bug in our collective software, rooted in our heritage of slavery, inspired by ignorance, and exorcised by the light of reason. As such racism could be moved to the margins of society through legal action and education until it might one day be eradicated. We have not yet figured out how to replace the functions that racism performed in making America operate effectively. Prejudice and racism have contributed positively to the functioning of society by strengthening the bonds between in-group members through ostracism of out-group members. Second, consider how a community might increase solidarity by refusing to allow outsiders access. Consider how much money, time and effort went toward maintaining separate and unequal educational systems prior to the civil rights movement. Consider the way slave owners justified slavery in the Antebellum South, by suggesting black people were functionally inferior to Whites and preferred slavery to freedom.

Prejudice and racism is functional to those in the dominant group, which means the group with power, privilege and social status. Obviously, both prejudice and racism have served the United States of America in order for it to exist as long as it has. Given the longevity, is it possible to reduce prejudicial attitudes in society? This perhaps could be a monumental task, given the history of racism and prejudice in America.

Racism in the United States of America has existed since the colonial era. Americans were given legally and socially sanctioned privileges and rights, while these same rights were denied to other races and minorities. European Americans, particularly affluent white Anglo-Saxon Protestants, have enjoyed exclusive privileges in matters of education, immigration, voting rights, citizenship, land acquisition and fair criminal procedures throughout American history.

On the contrary, black adult males are 5.9 times as likely to be incarcerated than Whites, and Hispanics are 3.1 times as likely. Further, despite this illusion of fairness in the criminal justice system, black men are sentenced to 20% more time for committing the exact same crime as a white man. According to a study by the Brookings Institution and the Pew Research Center, these disparities were observed "after controlling for a wide variety of sentencing factors, including age, education, citizenship, weapon possession and prior criminal history." Further, judges are less likely to voluntarily revise sentences downward for black offenders than for white ones. And even when judges do reduce black offenders' sentences, they do so by smaller amounts than for white offenders.

Let's take a look at a notoriety case that reflects the grossly obvious unfairness in sentencing inequality: Ethan, a 22-year-old Texas resident. His legal saga began in 2013, when he plowed his father's truck into a group of people helping a motorist on a Texas roadside, killing four people. Ethan was then 16, drunk, and had traces of the anti-anxiety drug valium in his blood. In the criminal case, Ethan's defense team argued that the teenager was spoiled as a child and that his wealthy upbringing prevented him from understanding the full consequences of his actions. His psychologist testified that Ethan suffered from "affluenza," which means having financial privilege. Keep in mind that this diagnosis is not recognized as a diagnostic category by the American Psychiatric Association (DSM-5). His psychologist argued for substance abuse treatment rather than jail time. Ultimately, a judge sentenced Ethan to 10 years of probation, ordering him to remain drug and alcohol free during that period. Ethan pleaded guilty to manslaughter and assault while intoxicated. In December 2015, a video surfaced on social media showing Ethan drinking. In an attempt to avoid prosecution, Ethan and his mother fled to Mexico, but were eventually tracked down. Ethan was sentenced to two years in jail for probation violation and was released in April 2018 after spending 720 days in a county jail, which basically amounts to 180 days for each of the four people he killed. On January 2nd, 2020, Ethan was arrested again and is currently being held without bond for testing positive for THC in a mandatory drug test that was part of his probation. Needless to say, this driving crash fueled fierce debate over the role of unfairness in the criminal justice system. There is a delusion of fairness in the criminal justice system, but, in actuality, the color of justice is green. In the United States of America, holding racist views can benefit those who want to deny rights and privileges to people they perceive as inferior to them, but, over time, this harms society.

In South Africa, it was functional for the white government to insist on maintaining apartheid because to do otherwise would mean that Whites would become a minority group in a black dominated society. The outcome of race-based disenfranchisement such as poverty, high crime, and discrepancies in employment and educational opportunities illustrates the long-term and clearly negative results of slavery and prejudicial attitudes in America. According to the functionalist theorist Parson, "The primary historic origin of the modern color problem lies in the relation of Europeans to African slavery." Slavery was beneficial to slaveholders and society. Parson is not denying that prejudice is produced through interactions. Rather, he is pointing out that the specific forms taken by those interactions, such as the oppression, subordination, and domination of Africans by Whites, is directly related to the perceived need of white colonialists and traders to use Africans for their own purposes. For example, slavery offered the South a practical and effective means of developing an agricultural economy based on cotton. Slaves provided a free labor force to work long hours, and the job required only physical endurance. This system worked, leaving slave owners free for leisure pursuits, while reaffirming in their minds the "inferiority" of their toiling "darkies."

A generation later, Jim Crow laws once again formalized a system of inequality through all social institutions. Many, though not all, middle-class non people of color, especially those that live in segregated communities, like to think that they got to where they are today by virtue of their merit, hard work, intelligence, and maybe a little luck. And while many may be sympathetic to the plight of others, we close down when we hear the words "affirmative action" or "racial preference." What we don't like to acknowledge is that preferences have a long institutional history in this country — a white history. For example, when slavery ended, its legacy lived on, not only in the impoverished conditions of black people, but in the wealth and prosperity that accrued to white slave owners and their descendants. Many economists who try to place a dollar value on how much White Americans have profited from 250 years of unpaid labor, coupled with nearly a century-long Jim Crow segregation of African Americans, including interest, begin their estimates at $10 to $20 trillion dollars. Rather than recognize how "racial preferences" have tilted the playing field and given white America a head start in life, instead, Black Americans are chastised for not achieving what non people of color have; we even invert the situation and accuse Black Americans of using "the race card" to advance themselves. Accusing a Black American of "playing the race card" when they speak about racism is intended to silence, threaten or shame someone into not mentioning the obvious racism they're being subjected to. Prejudice, conflict and strife appear to be basic elements of American society, as opposed to harmony, integration, and smooth functioning.

Chapter 4
Dehumanizing labels: A lifetime sentence

Labeling others is common in our society. Once a person or group has been labeled by others, it is common for that person to incorporate that label into his or her own self-concept. A person develops a stigma or a powerful negative label that greatly changes his or her self-identity. In this chapter, we will discuss the specifics of labeling theory, including when and why people are labeled. Labeling causes selective perceptions, that is, it leads us to see certain things while it blinds us to others. For example, if we apply a label to a group, we tend to perceive that its members are all alike. Racial and ethnic labels are very powerful. The behavior of these individuals may be determined or influenced by the terms used to describe or classify them. This classification is associated with the self-fulfilling prophecy and crime, which infers that people come to identify with and behave in ways that reflect how others see them. Further, labeling someone a criminal can cause others to treat them more negatively.

During my employment as a counselor at a correctional detention facility, part of my job entailed teaching psycho-educational classes to inmates. One of the classes that was mandated was Thinking for Change, which is a cognitive behavioral curriculum developed by the National Institute of Corrections. The class focused on changing criminogenic thinking. Many of the inmates spoke openly about their inability to move forward in their lives after release. Despite the fact of having served their time for crimes committed, it was very difficult to reintegrate back into the community. The label of criminal remained attached to them, despite changing their behavior.

The definitions of criminality and deviance are established by those in power. The formation of laws and the interpretation of those laws by law enforcement, courts and correctional institutions are crucial reminders to offenders. Moreover, these institutions are tasked with enforcing standards of normalcy and labeling certain behaviors. By applying labels to people and creating categories of deviance, officials in these institutions are reinforcing society's power structure. Often, the dominant group in society defines deviance for poor men and women, the elderly, the young, and racial and ethnic minorities. The United States has the highest incarceration rate in the world. The American criminal justice system holds roughly 2.3 million inmates in state prisons, federal prisons, juvenile correctional facilities, local jails, military prisons, immigration detention facilities, civil commitment centers and state psychiatric hospitals.

According to statistics, African American males are at greater risk than their white counterparts of being arrested by the time they are young adults. A recent study indicated that by the time African American males reach age 22, nearly half of them have experienced an arrest. An arrest record is a permanent record that marks individuals as a criminal, and this changes the way institutions treat them. Another obstacle that inmates face upon being released back into the community is being denied employment and voting rights. Being a criminal becomes a person's status in life. Their criminal record (rap sheet) controls the way they are identified in public.

Society is enacted in the momentary situational encounters that humans perform with one another. In other words, there is no society independent of the human mind and human expression of culture. This implies that in a strict theoretical sense, humans exist as embryonic potential, and anything that the mind can conceive is possible. Labeling others is a social construct of reality. Therefore the relevant questions to ask are: How does society influence individual actions? And how does an individual's actions shape society?

Our court system distinguishes between those who are capable of knowing what the rules of society are and those who are deemed incompetent to stand trial because they do not comprehend the rules. The criminally insane are judged "unsocial." The rest of us are judged to be competent players because we know the rules of our society and are capable of directing our behavior accordingly. Regardless of whether we choose to obey or disobey the law, we have a choice.

Symbolic interaction takes the position that knowledge, including scientific knowledge, is relative. It is the product of the context within which it is constructed. Humans do not experience the world in its natural state. We do not gather and observe "facts" that interpret themselves. The selection and interpretation of data is based on classification schemes constructed by the observers. For example, many children engage in activities such as breaking windows, stealing fruit from other people's trees, climbing into other people's yards, or being truant from school. In affluent neighborhoods, these acts may be interpreted by parents, teachers and law enforcement as innocent aspects of growing up. On the other hand, in poor neighborhoods, these same acts would be considered criminal. Another example of a labeling double standard: research has shown that black girls and boys are disciplined more frequently and more harshly by teachers and school administrators than their peers of other races. However, there is no evidence to suggest that they misbehave more frequently. This suggests that social class plays an important role in labeling as well. Similarly and with much more severe consequences, statistics show that police officers kill Black Americans at a higher rate than Whites, even when they are unarmed and have not committed a crime. This suggests that the misapplication of deviant labels is a result of racial stereotypes at play.

Social observers have, for decades, commented on and demonstrated the ways in which stigmatized social groups and outsiders may fall victim to self-fulfilling cultural stereotypes. All too often, it is the victims who are blamed for their own plight, rather than the social expectations that have constrained their behavioral options.

Our perception of reality is related to our culture. Through our culture, we learn how to perceive the world around us. Cultural definitions such as deviance help us interpret the sensory stimuli from our environment and tell us how to respond to them. Culture is learned behavior acquired through verbal communication or language. A word is nothing more than a symbol that stands for something else. Whether it is tangible or intangible, the word represents a mental concept that is based on empirical reality. Because words symbolically interpret the world to us, the linguistic relativity of language may connote both intended and unintended prejudicial meanings. For example, black is the symbol of darkness or evil and white symbolizes cleanliness or goodness, and a society may subtly or not so subtly transfer these meanings to black and white people. William Theorem states that, "Once observed, if people define situations as real, those situations become real in their consequences." His statement is further testimony to the truth of reality constructs such as labeling.

Human beings respond to the definitions of stimuli rather than the stimuli themselves. People often associate images with specific minority groups. They then behave according to the meaning they assign to the situation, and the consequences of their behavior serve to reaffirm the meaning. The definition becomes a self-fulfilling prophecy. When Whites define Blacks as inferior and then offer them fewer opportunities because of their alleged inferiority, Blacks become disadvantaged, which, in turn — supports the initial definition. Moreover, when a particular racial or ethnic group commits a noticeable number of deviant offenses, such as delinquency, public drunkenness or some public nuisance problem, the public often extends a negative image to all members of that group, even if it applies to only a few. Debates about people who have committed crimes are littered with epithets. We label people as offenders, criminals, convicts, and lawbreakers. We label those who spend time in prison jailbirds. And we call those who've completed their sentences ex-offenders, ex-convicts and ex-cons. We also apply more specific epithets to people for particular offenses such as thief, murderer, and rapist. Even conscientious newspapers use these labels. In many other social areas, we have moved away from this kind of labeling, such as "the retarded." We now see just how prejudiced these labels are.

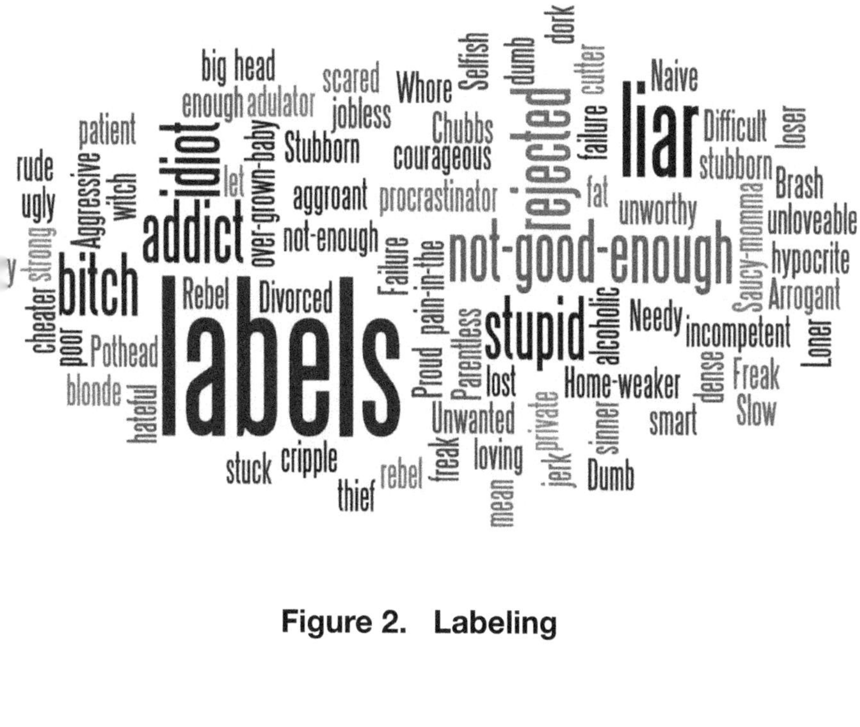

Figure 2. Labeling

All too often when beliefs create reality, it is the victims who are blamed for their own plight rather than the social expectations that have constrained their behavioral options.

We must recognize that giving people such labels hides the real complexity of their situation and limits their ability to shape their own lives.

Chapter 5

Rationalizing subordination

Throughout the 20th century, people of color, Blacks specifically, have made significant strides towards autonomy in American society, beginning with the right to own land and the right to vote, and the squelching of Jim Crow (American apartheid) segregation in southern states. These advances, however, appear to have not fully infiltrated the collective whole of American society. According to historian Ibram Kendi, racism, at its core, is a powerful system that creates false hierarchies of human value. "Its warped logic extends beyond race, from the way we treat people of different sexes, gender identities and body types." Kendi also stated that, "So many prominent Americans many of whom we celebrate for their progressive ideas and activism, many of whom had very good intentions subscribed to assimilationist thinking that has also served up racist beliefs about Black inferiority. They do so by promoting freedom but forgetting equality, by placing the burden of combating racism on black shoulders, not white ones; by implicitly accepting notions of inferiority no matter how righteous their indignation, by conflating anti-racist claims and racist fears in an effort to claim a moralizing middle ground. Strategies to undermine racism backfired." Kendi also argues that, "The subtext of respectability politics is that black people are partially responsible for the racist ideas directed at them because of how they act." These politics visibly embody their antithesis: if you're seen acting "respectably," they'll respect you. However, critics say that it's not an oppressed group's responsibility to answer for their own oppression.

The popular tools used for centuries to combat racism therefore are themselves racist. The supremacist ideologies and racist beliefs are still indoctrinated into Americans' psyche. These ideals that were ingrained in the mindset of Americans for so long have given way to a less conscious variant of segregation. And in Nicholas Guyatt's *Bind us Apart,* the author states that, "The most insidious assertion of American racism 'separate but equal' was more than a post reconstruction affirmation of Jim Crow laws, it was also a founding principle of the republic, one that still reverberates. As an adolescent growing up in Louisiana during that time, Blacks and Whites could eat at restaurants, or go to a movie theatre as long as they used different ones. Can separate ever be equal? Justice Marshall said it best, 'Segregation and inequality are equivalent concepts.' They have equal rating and equal footing. Furthermore, our country is proof that in almost all circumstances separate never means equal despite any well-meaning assurance that it does." The blatant practices such as hangings and beatings are no longer upheld by the law. Instead, it is a subtle practice that is the "crown jewel" of the entertainment media and film industries. It is the Paramount Pictures, NBCs, ABCs and Universal Studios of the world that are the propagators of negative stereotypes and escapable stigmas that many thought had been left behind. Whether it's appearing in disparaging roles or not appearing at all, minorities are the victim of an industry that relies on old ideas to appeal to the "majority at the expense of the significant minority." All blame, however, cannot be placed on the white males who run the industry, as a smaller number of black entertainers perpetuate these stereotypes as well. Despite defending their actions as an "insider look" into the life of a certain minority group, they are guilty of the same offenses that opponents have indicted the media, film and entertainment industries of propagating.

A picture can say a thousand words, according to Lippmann. By most historical accounts, Lippmann introduced the term "stereotype" to behavioral science in 1922. He used this term to represent the typical picture that comes to mind when thinking about a particular social group. In this chapter, we will describe the various mechanisms that help produce stereotypical perceptions, the complex interrelationship with prejudice and discrimination, and intergroup and interpersonal perception. We have tried to categorize them according to the primary nature of the process involved (cognitive, effective, socio-motivational and culturally). Despite some noteworthy early interest in the content of stereotypes (the process), they did not achieve mainstream status in psychology until the 1970s. This level of empirical interest would seem to suggest that stereotyping has important consequences for attitudes and behaviors toward social groups. Despite this initial functional view of stereotyping, early conceptions of stereotypes emphasized their flawed nature. Also asserted was the notion that stereotypes are products of faulty thought processes that led to largely incorrect beliefs. Many other theorists endorsed this approach, conceptualizing stereotypes as over generalizations resulting from irrational processes, and beliefs characterized by inordinate rigidity and resistance to change. Moreover, specific issues emphasized the role of erroneous causal perceptions, such as when stereotypes reflect attributions to racial rather than environmental causes, or when stereotypes are used to rationalize one's hostility toward a group.

Many studies have provided evidence that biased attributions about in groups and out groups are consistent features of social perception through early childhood. For example, people may make dispositional attributions, such as "lazy," to members of a group to provide a casual explanation for the group's disadvantaged economic status. Within the context of motivational desires to perceive groups in hierarchical relationships, stereotypic beliefs about groups often function to provide a rationale for and justification of status disparities, especially differences favoring the in group. A stereotype assumes that anyone in a particular group is very likely to have a certain characteristic.

American culture is full of stereotypes, such as the narrow-minded and greedy Jew, the lazy, musical, or sports-minded Black American, the hard-drinking Irish and the gang-prone Latino. Every one of these stereotypes, like all the others, is a gross overgeneralization. Undoubtedly, some people in any group may fit the stereotype, but many others do not. The point is not that stereotypes do not apply to anyone in the group at which they are aimed, but they are never true for everyone in that group. In addition, stereotypes are commonly reinforced by the film and entertainment industries. We will later explore the formation and function of stereotypes in these industries.

Keep in mind that stereotypes are viewed as being positive or negative. For example, undoubtedly it's good to be musical, athletic or a good dancer, which are common stereotypes about Black Americans. However, if Whites believe that these are the only areas in which Black Americans can achieve, then they will probably behave in ways that close off opportunities for Black Americans in professions other than sports and entertainment. Equally significant is that if young Black Americans internalize the message that the areas for them to get ahead are sports and music, they can be directed away from other areas in which they could be equally successful. Additionally, in the realm of racist thinking, as opposed to action, there are many definitions of prejudice.

However, in this book, prejudice has been conceptualized as involving a negative feeling or attitude toward the out group and an Inaccurate belief as well; it has both emotional and cognitive aspects. An example might be, "I hate Black and Mexican people because they smell worse than Whites." The first part of the sentence expresses the negative feelings (the hatred). The last part is an inaccurate generalization associated with a racial or ethnic category that goes beyond existing evidence. Why have Irish Americans long been stereotyped as lazy drunkards, Blacks as indolent, violent and oversexed, Italians as "mafia" types? Such questions force us to examine the role that prejudice and stereotypes play in the lives of individuals and groups. Conformity to prevailing beliefs is seen as a major source of prejudice. From this perspective, prejudices are not so much individually determined preferences, but, rather, shared social definitions of racial and ethnic groups. This points to the social adjustment function of prejudice. As a Southerner, I have witnessed numerous situations in which Northerners and Southerners have had to adjust to new racial beliefs as they moved from one region to another. Prejudice is a product of situations, not a little demon that emerges in people simply because they are depraved. These explanations partly explain why people hold prejudices and stereotypes; an additional factor mentioned earlier is that stereotypes help rationalize a subordinate group's position in society. When groups are subordinate, as in the case of white enslavement and exploitation of Black Africans, stereotypes developed, at least in part, to justify that subordination. When colonizers arrived on the continent of Africa, they could not explain their encounter with Africans. As such, they were racialized as ignorant and lazy. This characterization followed Africans to America and other parts of the world. Even in today's society with its history, in most societies, when individuals come into contact with others, they typically try to acquire information that will help them define the situation and make interaction easier. This goal is accomplished in part by attending to status cues. A sociologist developed this idea by studying the way Black Americans interact on streets in two adjacent urban neighborhoods. Members of both groups visually inspect strangers before concluding that they are not dangerous. They make assumptions about others on the basis of skin color, age, gender, companions, clothing, jewelry and the objects they carry with them. They evaluate the movements of strangers, the time of day, and other factors to establish how dangerous they might be. In general, children pass inspection easily. White women and white men are treated with greater caution, but not as much caution as Black American women and men. Apparently, urban dwellers are most suspicious of Black American male teenagers. People are most likely to interact verbally with individuals who are perceived as the safest.

Although status cues may be useful in helping people define the situation and thus greasing the wheels of social interaction, they also pose a social danger, for status cues can quickly degenerate into stereotypes, or rigid views of how members of various groups act, regardless of whether individual group members really behave that way. Stereotypes create social barriers that impair interaction or prevent it altogether. For example, law enforcement officers in some states routinely stop young Black American male drivers, without cause, to check for proper licensing, possession of illegal goods, and so forth. In this case, a social cue has become a stereotype that guides police policy. A great majority of Black Americans view this police practice as harassment. Racial stereotypes therefore help to perpetuate the sometimes poor relations between Black American communities and law enforcement officials. The distinction between affect and cognition has been an essential one in understanding racial bias in inter-group relations. As mentioned earlier, dual processing theories inform us that people tend to use existing stereotypical knowledge rather than individuating information while communicating with a member of another cultural group. Prior research demonstrates that cognition-based stereotypes are better predictors of participants' social judgements and policy opinions, and that affect-based prejudice is a better predictive of social distance and nonverbal communication. Moreover, in view of these contributions, it seems likely that group stereotypic knowledge structures have a substantial impact on perceptions of individuals belonging to salient identity groups.

Chapter 6
Social constructs of mass media stereotypes

Blacks have been treated as second-class citizens since the inception of the United States of America. Forcibly brought here as slaves to the "white man," Blacks have never been treated as completely equal to Whites. Stereotypes are rampant in today's society. These degrading stereotypes are reinforced and enhanced by the negative portrayal of Blacks in the media. Black characters have appeared in American films since the beginning of the industry. Stereotypes of Black Americans grew as a natural consequence of both scientific racism (which is a pseudoscientific belief that empirical evidence exists to support or justify racial superiority and discrimination) and legal challenges to both their personhood and citizenship. In an 1857 Supreme Court case, Fred Scott v. John F.A. Sandford,

Chief Justice Roger B. Taney dismissed the humanness of those of African descent. This legal precedent permitted the image of Black Americans to be reduced to caricatures in popular culture, with decades of old and current-day incarnations of Black American stereotypes, including Mammy, Uncle Tom, Sapphire, Watermelon and Mandingo. Many of the stereotypes created during the height of the trans-Atlantic slave trade were used to help commodify black bodies and justify the business of slavery. For instance, an enslaved person forced under violence to work from sunrise to sunset could hardly be described as lazy. Yet, laziness, as well as characteristics of submissiveness, backwardness, and lewdness, among others, were historically assigned to Black Americans.

The historical development of stereotyping and media application of these stereotypes in films are socially constructed. For example, the Mammy stereotype developed as an offensive racial caricature during slavery and was popularized through comic (black face) enactment of racial stereotypes. Enslaved black women were highly skilled domestic workers, working in the homes of white families as caretakers for their children. The pearl milling company's incarnation of the smiling domestic Aunt Jemima, which became synonymous with the "Mammy" figure, would also grow alongside the American oil industry. On the other hand, "Uncle Tom" was depicted as an innately submissive, obedient slave and in constant desire of the Whites' approval. The term became popular during the great migration when many southern born Blacks moved to northern cities like New York, Chicago and Detroit. With them, they brought codes of conduct expected in hostile Jim Crow environments.

The stereotype "Uncle Tom" was first publicly recorded during an address by Marcus Garvey, in 1919. The "Sapphire" caricature from the 1800s through to the mid 1900s portrayed black women as sassy, emasculating and domineering. Unlike the "Mammy" figure, the social construction of "Sapphire" depicted black women as aggressive, loud, and angry, which was perceived as an indirect violation of social norms. The "Sapphire" stereotype earned its name on the CBS television show "Amos and Andy" in 1951. In addition, "Watermelon" became a racist stereotype in the Jim Crow era. Before "Watermelon" became a stereotype, it symbolized self-sufficiency. Later, the fruit was turned into a symbol of poverty and a feast for the "unclean, lazy and child-like." As a means to shame black watermelon merchants, popular ads, including postcards, pictured Black Americans stealing, fighting over, or sitting in streets eating watermelon. Lastly, the black buck who was conjured up in the mind of slavers and auctioneers to promote the strength, breeding, ability and agility of muscular young black men, the "Mandingo" was born, a physically powerful black man brutally forced into labor. Emancipation brought with it fears that these men would exact sexual revenge against white men through their daughters, as depicted in the film "Birth of Nation." The reinforcement of the stereotype "Mandingo" as animalistic and brutish gave legal authority to white mobs and militias who tortured and killed black men for the safety of the public. Even today, the motion picture industry has not quite outgrown its immaturity. Blacks were not hired to portray Blacks in early works. Instead, white actors and actresses were hired to portray the characters with "blackface." By refusing to hire black actors to portray black characters, demeaning stereotypes were being created, as Blacks were presented in an unfavorable light. In addition, Blacks were purposely portrayed in films with negative stereotypes that reinforced white supremacy over Blacks. This has had a tremendous effect on America's view of Black Americans.

Unfortunately, the media sets the tone for the morals, values and images of our culture. Many people in America, some of whom have never encountered black people, may believe that the degrading stereotypes of Blacks are based on reality and not fiction. The media is powerful insofar as the social construction of reality. After over a century of movie making, these horrible stereotypes continue to plague our society today. As mentioned earlier, just as stereotypes can be positive or negative, prejudicial feelings can also be hostile or benevolent. Research shows that even seemingly positive stereotypes might not necessarily translate into positive attitudes toward out groups. For example, Asian Americans are perceived as intelligent, polite and model minorities. On the other hand, many are considered unsociable and lacking in communication skills, leading to ambivalent feelings toward them. In other words, affective and cognitive dimensions might not necessarily translate to favorable attitudes toward out groups.

In recent history, progress has been made in the way in which minorities are portrayed on television. The unanimous declaration that television is very influential, especially in the adoption of beliefs in children, has caused a flurry of changes to take place. Despite these changes, however, there are obstacles we must overcome before everything is the way it should be. These obstacles include ratings, and, more importantly, the people at the top who decide on programming. Until this changes, the progress will remain slow, and, at times, nonexistent.

There are still far too many shows that portray minorities in negative ways and too few that show reality. Television has the capacity to disseminate information to millions of people in a way that no other medium of exchange can match. As a result, mass media has become increasingly entwined with television and less to do with newspapers, magazines and other print sources. Television, whether it's news, sitcoms or dramas, often gives people insight into worlds that are unfamiliar and vastly different from their own. In fact, television can be the only exposure that some people have regarding racial and ethnic groups. Television is extremely important, as it is possible to heavily influence the thoughts and beliefs of a large number of impressionable viewers, most notably, children, who most often have no frame of reference. The public is concerned about the issue of media diversity, as it is generally accepted that mass media has strong social and psychological effects on viewers. For example, film and television provide many children with their first exposure to people of other races, ethnicities, religions, and cultures. What they see on the screen can impact their attitudes about the treatment of others. Many studies support this contention, and, in turn, should illustrate the importance of social responsibility that those in power have to ensure that television portrays people of color accurately and without bias.

The United States of America is one of the most culturally diverse countries in the world but the media and entertainment industries tell a completely different story. Because television is such an integral part of society, it is imperative that the wrong ideas and values do not go across the airwaves into the homes of young children. According to a report titled "Reality in Television," studies have shown that television teaches stereotypical perceptions about people that they would have no contact with outside of watching the way these people are shown by television. Unfortunately, children spend lots of time watching television unsupervised, and, in essence, the television becomes the teacher. Children are most likely unable to distinguish a stereotype from reality. Once these stereotypes and misconceptions become ingrained in the minds of American children, they become self-perpetuating. Minorities, such as Latinos and Black Americans, are the casualty of a media that perpetuates social stereotypes. Essentially, the media is portraying a biased view of society and therefore not promoting the aim of presenting the public with an objective coverage.

Movies, television, and the news are all guilty of what most people would consider racist beliefs. The marginal progress that has been made in the industry, coupled with decades of reform, should produce results significantly more substantial than those that they have witnessed. Moreover, as a society, we need to take an introspective look at ourselves and realize that, in order for us to achieve our eventual aims, we must not give in to the monetary benefits of producing self-disparaging movies and television shows. Do we continue on the same path that we have paved for ourselves or do we take a more proactive role and diverge from the established path and pave a new road? In light of the industry's sloth-like environment, these are questions that must be presented to society.

This proves to be a very difficult environment to introduce multicultural programming. People inherently cast those who look like them in professional roles and roles that are looked upon positively. And, of course, when it comes time to cast a role that is looked upon negatively, people tend to cast people in it who don't look like themselves. Is this a conscious behavior? Probably not, but it will take a conscious effort to reverse this trend that lends itself to stereotyping and racism. To say that the problem of portraying minorities negatively is as bad now as it was in the past is inaccurate, but to say that the situation was good would also be just as grossly inaccurate. We must recognize that there are changes that need to be made and there are barriers that stand in the way of change. The only way to remove these barriers is to persist in what you believe is right. Don't get me wrong! Yes, there are shows that portray people of color positively, but there are still far too many that place people of color in inferior roles. Until television represents reality, it will be a threat to those who are uninformed and impressionable. But for now, change is occurring, and hopefully it will pick up the pace in the future.

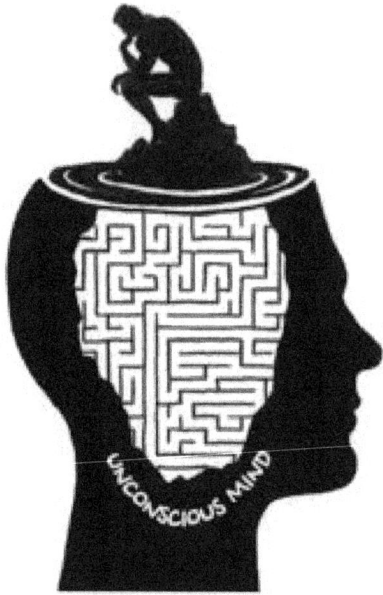

Figure 3. Unconscious Bias

Understanding racial bias in inter-group relations provides an account of how thought can arise in two different ways. The two processes consist of an implicit bias (unconscious process) and an explicit (controlled conscious) process. This informs us that people tend to use existing stereotypical knowledge rather than individuation information which helps define a person as an individual, rather than as a member of a group.

Chapter 7
Humanity:
Whatever affects one directly affects all indirectly

The fact that many people hold stereotypical ideas about other groups may be an indication that they are prejudiced. But this fact does not imply that they will actually discriminate against people whom they perceive as different. Prejudice is an attitude; discrimination is a behavior. Many people are prejudiced and discriminate against members of particular groups. There are also people who are not prejudiced but who discriminate because it is expected of them, such as in the case of institutional racism, whereby discrimination is embedded in the fabric of society. For example, the disproportionate number of black men arrested, charged and convicted of crimes may reflect racial profiling, a form of institutional racism. Discrimination also consists of actions against a group of people. It can be based on age, religion, health, and other indicators; race-based laws against discrimination strive to address this set of social problems.

Discrimination based on race or ethnicity can take many forms, such as unfair housing practices, or biased hiring systems. Overt discrimination has long been part of U.S. history. In the late 19th century, it was common for business owners to hang up signs that read, "Help wanted: Whites only," and these signs exemplified overt discrimination that is not tolerated today. However, we cannot erase past discrimination from our culture just by enacting laws to abolish it. Sociologist Emile Durkheim calls racial discrimination a social fact, meaning that it does not require the action of the individual to continue. The reasons are very complex, as they relate to the educational, criminal, economic and political systems in our society. For example, when a newspaper identifies individuals by race when accused of a crime, this may enhance stereotypes of a certain minority.

Prejudice and discrimination does overlap in many ways. To illustrate, let's take a look at these examples. Unprejudiced non discriminators are generally open minded, tolerant and accepting individuals. Prejudiced non discriminators are those who hold racist beliefs but don't act on them, such as racist businesses which serve minority customers. Prejudiced discriminators include those who actively make disparaging remarks about others or who perpetuate hate crimes. Discrimination also manifests in different ways. The examples above are examples of individual discrimination, but there are other types.

Institutional discrimination occurs when a society has developed an embedded disenfranchisement of a group. On the other hand, institutional discrimination can also include the promotion of a group's status, such as the case of "white privilege," which is the benefits people receive simply by being part of the dominant group. The problem associated with white privilege is that many, though not all "white" people are willing to admit that non white people live with a set of disadvantages due to their skin color, but very few are willing to acknowledge the benefits they receive as a result of being in a dominant group. Institutional discrimination can be very deliberate, as in the system of previous school segregation and denial of voting rights to Blacks that existed throughout the U.S. South until the early 1960s.

However, we are seeing today, in 2020, voter suppression efforts, such as politicians passing measures making it harder for Black Americans and other people of color to cast a ballot. The goal behind this is to manipulate the outcome. Also, in the educational system, for example, teachers often expect less achievement from black and Hispanic students than they do from white students, according to a study by Brophy College. Another important example of institutional discrimination is the movement of jobs out of predominantly black and Hispanic central cities and into predominantly white suburbs. This trend, according to studies, takes job opportunities away from the minority groups and gives them to Whites. This evidence shows that where jobs have become suburbanized in this manner, black and Hispanic men have higher unemployment rates than white men.

The relationship between stereotypes (prejudice) and discrimination is not always clear. However, sociologist Merton has shown in his typology that everyone that is prejudiced does not discriminate. With these distinctions in mind, a typology of prejudice was constructed (see Figure 4). This typology is valuable because it points to the variety of attitudes and behaviors that exist in multicultural and multiracial societies. However, the typology fails to account for situations in which certain groups are discriminated against, regardless of the attitudes and behaviors of individuals. This form of discrimination is part of the "culture" of a social institution and is practiced by people who are simply conforming to the norms of those institutions.

Social pressure and the costs of discriminating or not discriminating determine whether racial attitudes will be translated into behavior. If an imposed cost were attached to discrimination, such as legal hearings and penalties, prejudiced people will often not discriminate. Similarly, unprejudiced people may discriminate if pressured to do so if they are losing white customers. Recent research shows that stereotypes among Whites are an important cause of discrimination against Black Americans in employment and in housing. It is evident that discrimination and stereotypes are a crucial part of everyday adaptation to the social world. Yet, many insist that it is a distortion of reality in that it represents a failure to appreciate the way people really are: unique, differentiated and disparate individuals. The criteria developed in an attempt to assess the "reality" of these perceptions are necessarily confounded because the criteria by which stereotypes are measured are based on perception.

TYPOLOGY OF PREJUDICE

PREJUDICE

Yes	No
True Bigot	Weak Liberal
Does not believe in the American creed and acts accordingly.	Not prejudiced, yet afraid to go against the bigoted crowd.
Cautious Bigot	Strong Liberal
Does not believe in the American creed, but is afraid to discriminate.	Not prejudice and refuses to discriminate.

Figure 4. Typology chart of prejudice

Chapter 8
We choose our attitude

From the time that stereotypes were introduced into the social sciences, they were considered to represent attitudes related to prejudice or authoritarianism. However, once theorists began assessing the qualities of stereotypes empirically, the situation became unclear. Moreover, it has not been determined whether stereotypes do, in fact, represent attitudes or even if they are related to attitudes towards the stereotyped group. Further, it is possible that these constructs covary to a certain degree, while also maintaining some independence. Some ethnic stereotypes may be shared across individuals of varying attitudes toward the ethnic group, while others may be systematically related to how one feels about the ethnic group and therefore may not be shared by all. In the following

97

review, an attempt is made to demonstrate that stereotypes and attitudes are different constructs.

Racial or ethnic attitudes may be associated with the content of individuals' stereotypes of an ethnic or racial group. Although much of the literature on this topic either directly or indirectly indicates that attitudes lead to stereotypes (prejudice), it is possible that stereotypical perceptions themselves create one's attitude. The casual order between these constructs, however, has not been investigated. In early research, evidence indicated that consensual stereotypes (prejudice) or uniformity within the respondent's base have little or no relation to group preferences.

In other words, trait descriptions that met with uniformity or agreement within the sample population were not related to general feelings toward the group the traits described. In addition, Brigham suggested that degrees of stereotyping did not correlate with attitudes towards Blacks. Brigham has reported, however, that there were tendencies for specific trait attributions made by Whites about Blacks that are related to Whites' racial attitudes in his study. He indicated, though, that these specific traits were not necessarily stereotypical, as there was no relationship between uniformity (agreement) and favorableness of attitudes towards Blacks, and uniformity was a necessary criterion to stereotype in the paradigm used. These results are confused by the various criteria thought to be necessary for a trait ascription to be a stereotype, that is, consensus or uniformity within the entire sample population were necessary criteria for something to be called a stereotype. Given the definition of stereotype endorsed in this book, it is possible that those traits are stereotypical for some and not for others.

More specifically, it is postulated here that subgroups of the sample population who have negative racial attitudes may hold different stereotypes than subgroups of individuals with less negative or more positive racial attitudes. When considering this possibility, it is clear that no trait is unconditionally a stereotype of a given group but traits may be stereotypical according to different subgroups' perceivers. Given the findings reported thus far, there is evidence that individuals with different attitudes towards an ethnic or racial group may also hold some different stereotypes about that group.

It appears that attitudes and stereotypes are likely related, such as the fact that those with negative attitudes toward a group tend to hold more negatively evaluative stereotypes of that group, in addition to others more commonly adhered to. In support of this contention, Vinacke suggests that, "It is probably not the fact of stereotyping per se, which marks the prejudiced person, so much as the content of the stereotypes and how they are used." Further, he suggests that the content of the stereotype of persons high or low in prejudice may be different. For example, it is likely that prejudiced persons possess stereotypes with different evaluative tones to those of non prejudiced individuals. The study also found that while there was equal knowledge of stereotypes and labels typically used in describing Blacks, they were significantly different in content for those high in prejudice as compared to those low in prejudice. It follows then that stereotypes held (believed or adhered to) by these groups may be different.

Figure 5. Inclusion

The concept of equality for all in our legal system does not support differences, it only supports sameness. We will be free only when we are respected and accepted for our differences and the diversity we provide to this society.

Chapter 9
Interpersonal contact

One of the most obvious functions of language is the transmission of culturally shared stereotypes from person to person and from generation to generation. Because language is culturally shared, it provides an ideal means of collectively defining and preserving stereotypic beliefs. Most general levels of culturally shared beliefs are wired into the vocabulary of a given language. A child growing up at a given time in a given culture acquires a lexicon that reflects these stereotypical beliefs. For example, depending on the decade in which an American grew up, he or she learned to refer to dark-skinned citizens as "Nigger," "Negro," "Black" or "Afro-American." These terms imply very different qualities and evoke very different images and associations.

Can stereotypical perceptions change? Yes, they can change, and we will focus this chapter around how to change Whites' attitudes and stereotypical perceptions by way of interracial interpersonal contact.

The potential limitations in the generalizability of my conclusion to other types of intergroup relations was done for several reasons. First, the relationship between Blacks and Whites has been an enduring issue throughout much of the history of the United States. How we think is influenced by our culture; the ways that we interact are changed by how we think and feel. Arguably, the intergroup contact hypothesis formalized by Allport has been the single most influential scientific framework concerned with prejudice reduction. The contact theory maintains that the sharp spatial social gulf between the social lives of "Whites" and "Blacks" promotes a lack of awareness about Blacks. This lack of awareness feeds stereotypical perceptions which are erroneous oversimplified negative beliefs about Blacks. This, in turn, engenders feelings of hostility and discriminatory social dispositions towards Blacks.

Stouffer introduced the contact theory in his book, *The American Soldier*. This experimental study represents one of the first known attempts to empirically test the contact theory of prejudice. The study reported positive effects on Whites' racial attitudes, although the generality of the attitudes to broader social situations was sometimes questionable. Further, in the analysis of behavior and attitudes, the studies revealed that proximity had a pronounced positive effect on the level of informal interaction and friendship with Blacks. According to Stouffer, the relation between intergroup contact and attitude change is not likely to be generalized to other situations unless the individuals have close interpersonal relationships with members of the other group in real-life situations. The contact theory is an important contribution to the field because it pays careful attention to Whites' interracial contact and the effect that position has on the development of racial attitudes. The importance of developing a variety of contacts with Blacks is congruent with the contact theory.

However, the same cannot be said of the apparent unimportance of intimacy (such as with personal friends), which is motivationally compelling. The study asserts that to be effective in bringing Whites into personal contact with Blacks, the contact should not take place within a competitive context. Second, the contact must be sustained rather than episodic. Third, the contact must be personal, informal, and one on one. Finally, the setting in which the contact occurs must confer equal status on both parties, rather than duplicate the racial status differential. Most interracial contact does not meet these conditions. Consider, for example, the contact between white and black neighbors who pass each other daily on the street without personal interaction or between black and white employees who work together. These forms of contact are considered insufficient to remove Whites' blinders and allow them to perceive Blacks in a fresh light. In contrast, the contact that occurs between intimate personal friends appears to meet optimally the conditions of the contact theory.

A Caribbean American professor was asked in an interview with race and ethnic relations authors this question: "How do you personally feel being black in a mostly white society and workplace?" The professor stated, "I usually interact with White Americans from a distance. Most are acquaintances, not friends. I am not invited to their informal gatherings. The occasional exchanges in our hallway are only superficial. My differences are neither acknowledged nor respected."

Due to social norms, everyone is expected to move in the same direction. The denial of our cultural differences is a perfect tool to keep others, and Blacks, in particular, within the boundaries of America's cultural definition. While the contact theory developed primarily out of a policy oriented concern with proposals to reduce prejudice, its central tenets rest on important assumptions about the very nature of intergroup attitudes and racial stereotypes. Thus, negative intergroup attitudes are prejudiced attitudes that have an irrational basis and are permeated by feelings of hostility. This fundamental assumption has important corollaries, in that people who interact with one another in society take one another into account as they communicate, take on roles, and cooperate. Similarly they share an understanding of reality, and hence develop a set of rules by which to live. By the same token, by its very nature, they cut off interaction with those outside that interaction. This exclusion is the basis for racial problems in this country, and is the basis for similar problems in most societies. The United States of America has developed two Americas with several distinctive identities, and thus, in a basic sense, is not as united as it appears. We are currently facing a re-emergence of racial conflict in our society. Without continuous interaction between the majority and minorities in the United States, people will fail to communicate with and understand each other. Role taking and cooperation between them will be minimized. People in the dominant society (Whites), through interaction, can develop a perspective that is useful for their understanding of reality, and include in their definition of those in the other society (minorities), the reason for their differences as well as justification for the inequality that exists between Blacks and Whites. If people do not regularly interact, communicate and cooperate with each other, no shared culture is likely to develop.

Studies have suggested that familiarity (exposure) and interracial contact with the target group should have a positive association, such as reducing prejudice, decreasing the negativity of stereotypes, and increasing the accuracy of stereotypes. This contention is a general basis of the contact theory and the anticipated positive effects of a well integrated society. Accordingly, the evidence of association between interracial contact and racial attitudes has been mixed.

Positive results have been contingent upon the amount and type of contact exposure. Moreover, a cooperative atmosphere, supportive of egalitarian norms or settings that promote intimacy, are among other factors. Likewise, most researchers acknowledge that increased exposure or contact under circumstances without these qualities may serve to reinforce traditional negative attitudes and stereotypes of ethnic groups. Therefore, contact or exposure is not a panacea, but intergroup contact that includes some of the above-noted characteristics may effect a change in social perceptions.

Studies show that there were as many positive findings as there were negative findings with regard to the impact of interracial contact upon racial attitudes. The issue, however, is who, in everyday living, is exposed to interracial interactions under the conditions specified in the contact theory? This issue is especially important for those who have prejudicial attitudes, because such attitudes enter into how a person interprets such encounters. The evidence supports that a prejudiced person "is uninformed about the way out-group members [Blacks] behave and the way in-group members [Whites] should behave toward them." This lack of information reportedly increases anxiety at the mere prospect of having to interact with a person of another racial or ethnic group. The prejudiced individual(s) tend to avoid interracial interaction, which creates less opportunity to alter racial attitudes and mediate the outcomes of such contact when "exposed" to members of the other group. Some individuals, especially prejudiced individuals, will likely have typical superficial interactions for the most part. In addition, it is postulated that those with negative racial attitudes may keep their attitudes intact by avoiding interracial contact, and that racial attitudes raise the possibility of self-selection. There is no doubt that something as personal as one's circle of friends reflects one's own choices and is not a factor that is out of one's control. It is a given fact that many Whites would prefer to avoid or minimize their contacts with Blacks. However, economic and political concerns constrain individuals to take a job regardless of the presence of Blacks in the workplace and in neighborhoods.

Society often expresses the opinion that specific traits of members in certain groups are responsible for their disadvantaged situation, which is grounded in stereotypical perceptions and lack of contact. As mentioned earlier, it is common in the United States of America to assert that Black Africans weren't ready for full citizenship because "they remain childlike and simple." These stereotypical explanations are inflexible images within a category invoked by the individual to justify or deny "white privilege." As previously stated, negative inter-group attitudes are prejudiced attitudes that have an irrational bias and are permeated by feelings of hostility. This fundamental assumption has three important corollaries. First, intergroup attitudes are interpreted primarily as a property of individuals, and researchers were drawn by individual-level variations in attitudes toward Blacks and attempted to account for that variation by examining individual differences in personality, socialization and interracial experiences. The contact theory focused on the latter as a potential policy tool. Second, if negative inter-group attitudes are founded in irrationality and misinformation, the way to positive attitudes is with rationality and correct information. There are no serious

114

differences that exist between Blacks and Whites, and thus more exposure under the conditions of the contact theory will reveal the falsity of negative beliefs about Blacks. Third, because discriminatory behavioral predispositions toward Blacks reflect a feeling of antipathy, the way to nondiscriminatory predispositions is to generate positive feelings towards Blacks. In essence, the problem of racial prejudice is the individual's erroneous generalizations and the connection between personal feelings of antipathy and discriminatory predispositions. These all point logically to the probable efficacy of situations that would foster close personal friendships between Blacks and Whites.

Allport argued that the effects of proximity and personal contact are mutually dependent and reinforcing in that each must be present for the other to have an effect. Proximity does not have a direct effect of its own on racial attitudes when personal contact accompanies it, and the more personal contact there is, the greater the effect of proximity. Further, it appears that personal contact needs to be backed up by physical proximity to Black Americans if it is to influence Whites' racial attitudes. And the more sustained the proximity, the greater the impact of personal contact. The stipulations of the contact theory infer that interracial contact cannot offset the status differential between Whites and Black Americans, as this is embedded in the fabric of American society. The significance of experiencing a variety of extended interracial contact cannot be underestimated. Therefore, social policies that encourage individuals of diverse backgrounds to interact with another in a variety of settings should be promoted whenever feasible, such as in schools, workplaces, and the community.

Most Whites who have contact with Black Americans experience only "token" contact. This refers to a perfunctory effort of symbolic gesture toward accomplishing racial integration. Given this perspective, the empirical relationship between contact and Whites' racial attitudes presents a different issue than that posed by the contact theory. The issue is that such intrinsic facts invade the boundaries of intimate friendship. For example, the pervasive force of societal defined inequalities determines the predisposition of the individual. A relationship between Black Americans and Whites not marked by historical discrimination, racism and inequality would perhaps be a different relationship from the one with which American society is confronted today.

It would seem fair to state that most studies show that true acquaintance lessens prejudice. One important qualification must be noted, and that is that prejudice is reflected in both beliefs and attitudes. It seems highly probable that increased knowledge of a minority group would lead directly to a truer set of beliefs. It does not follow, however, that attitudes will change proportionately. For example, plenty of rationalizations for prejudice are available to people who have a reasonable amount of sound knowledge. For the sake of caution, this chapter concludes as follows: Interracial contact that brings knowledge and acquaintance is likely to engender sounder beliefs concerning minority groups, and, for this reason, can contribute to the reduction of prejudice. Moreover, it's also fair to state that interracial contact cannot always overcome prejudicial attitudes, as this may be deep-rooted in the character structure of the individual. The issue of who in everyday living is exposed to interracial contact under the conditions specified in the contact theory is important. This issue is especially important because those who have prejudicial attitudes will determine how such persons interpret their encounters. For example, there is a lack of accurate information about Blacks in America. Without getting to know each other, there is a tendency to fill in the blanks with little reflection.

Several social scientists, including this author, agree that the trend of evidence favors the conclusion that contact has been shown to be of utmost importance in reduction of prejudice and promoting positive intergroup attitudes. The work on interracial contact highlights the importance of equal status between the groups, and the importance of positive media presentations of intergroup friendships. If these factors are implemented, they will, in turn, promote a more tolerant and truly integrated society.

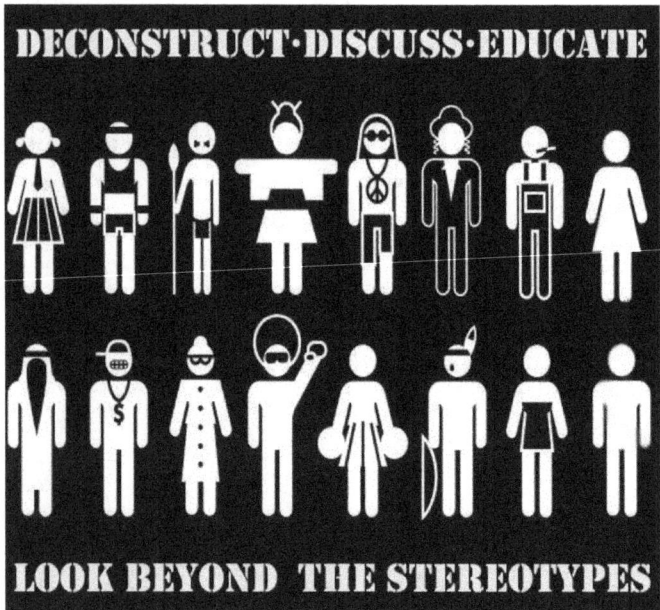

Figure 6.   Interracial Contact

In the absence of specific information we use general categories to impose meaning on people, and events to form judgement that we then rely on to guide our behavior. The untold story is how the ideas of "society" get into the human mind and influence individual perceptions.

Epilogue
Influencing social change

The ethical guidelines for human conduct were established millennia ago in the great creedal systems of humanity, all of them establishing the need and rationale for a people linked by a common interest: life, liberty and the pursuit of happiness. Our existence is tied to the interconnectedness that holds us and everything together. When we realize our inter-being and act mindfully on our awareness, we can be together with others with an open heart. The color of your skin should not matter, but the content of your character should. There are many faces that resemble each other, yet how easily we do not see and embrace others' uniqueness and identity. Imagine the ocean, which is a hole but has countless waves, each and every one different from all the others, and its currents, each unique and ever changing. The face of the United States of America is rapidly changing. Several of America's largest states have already crossed this threshold and more will do so in the next few decades. This demographic shift offers many benefits to the United States, such as expanding the labor force. By 2050, minorities would make up more than 50 percent of the population and become the majority. Increasing diversity could possibly make America a more hostile place. A study done by Craig and Richeson (2014) on interracial interactions indicated that when people are in the majority, the sense of their race is dormant. But the prospect of being in the minority can suddenly make white identity, and all the historical privilege that comes with it, salient.

As this country diversifies, many Americans, particularly non people of color, are choosing to self-segregate into racially isolated communities. White anxiety about a changing society will limit face-to-face contact, which is necessary to assuage their fears of living among people of color.

There may be no process more complex and intriguing than those by which strangers become friends. How do we form first impressions of the people we encounter? How do we become acquainted with each other? It is these and similar concerns that social psychologists have addressed in an attempt to chart the unfolding dynamics of social interaction and interpersonal relationships. Many studies have measured the ways in which first impressions channel and influence subsequent social interaction and acquaintance processes. For example, when we first meet others, we cannot help but notice certain highly visible and distinctive characteristics such as their sex, age, race, and bodily appearance. Social psychologists have said that realities are socially constructed and maintained through interaction. Moreover, empirical research has attempted to demonstrate that stereotypes may create their own social reality by channeling social interaction in ways that cause the stereotyped individual to behave in ways that conform to another person's stereotyped impression of him or her.

Another feature of reality constructs are beliefs which are self-fulfilling prophecies, which are assumptions or predictions that, purely as a result of having been made, cause the expected or predicted event to occur and thus confirm its own "accuracy." Self-fulfilling beliefs can have both positive and negative outcomes for the person who holds them. Often what is important is not what is factually correct, but what is defined as real. We've seen this example many times in the mass media and in people that embrace unsubstantiated information as factual. People act based on their definitions of what is real. For example, socially held beliefs about the characteristics of groups of people, in other words, stereotypes, often result in self-fulfilling outcomes.

How do we change our unconscious biases? According to historian and author Kendi, "In order to be truly antiracist you must oppose all the sexism, homophobia, colorism, ethnocentrism, nativism, cultural prejudice, and class bias teamed with racism that harm many Black lives" in a full-throated embrace of intersectionality. Moreover, theoretical and empirical research suggests that when perceivers have access to individuating information about stigmatized targets (people of color), they are less likely to display biases toward such individuals.

Jennifer Eberhardt has studied unconscious bias for years. She has discussed the "other race effect," in which people have trouble recognizing faces of other racial groups. For example, she stated in an interview that, "In Oakland California, a gang of black teenagers caused a mini crime wave of purse snatching among middle-aged women in Chinatown. When police asked the teens why they targeted that neighborhood, they said that Asian women, when faced with a line-up "couldn't tell black men apart." Eberhardt has written about the phrase "They all look alike." "There's no doubt that plenty of overt bigotry exists," but she has found that most of us harbor bias without knowing it. "It stems from the brain's tendency to categorize things — a useful function in the world but one that can lead to discrimination and baseless assumptions." Although scholars have long studied circumstances that shape prejudice, inquiry into factors associated with long-term prejudice reduction has been more limited.

When we speak about race and ethnic relations, you'll find that many but not all Americans agree that people of all races and ethnicities should be treated equally and with respect. However, personal experiences and news reports have painted a different story. People of color, specifically, Black Americans, are aware that racial prejudice has a major impact on our lives and on our community. Prejudice alone does not fully account for all racial dynamics, including occurrences where people of color may experience different treatment from white people. We must also come to terms with the impact of racial anxiety — the discomfort people feel in anticipation of or during interracial interactions. Many of us may be concerned about how we may be perceived when we are communicating with others who come from different racial groups or ethnicities. In addition, the subject of race may be particularly severe, as people of color worry that they will fall victim to racial bias, and white people may worry that their words or actions will be misconstrued or assumed to be racist. This anxiety very often comes from a lack of experience in interacting with or being around other racial groups, and this leads us to develop cultural stereotypes or distorted perceptions (biases) about what other groups are like.

However, and fortunately, racial anxiety is something that can be changed. This would require us to reach beyond our segregated friendship circles or communities and develop meaningful relationships with people of color, and Black Americans, specifically. This has been proven by psychological research. Keep in mind that the advantage of interracial contact may not occur right away; one brief meeting between strangers or acquaintances can induce anxiety, especially for those with a brief history of interracial experiences. It is projected that people usually become more comfortable with one another through repeated interactions across cultures that will grow closer with time. According to research, this happens even among people that show high levels of racial bias. Moreover, the contact theory states that reduced prejudice happens most often when people from different races work together as equals towards a common goal. Institutional support that endorses this kind of equal status also helps a great deal. However, such favorable conditions can't always be guaranteed across different situations. We can use cooperative learning strategies to help create a common sense of identity and increase the potential for members from different groups to become friends. We can do this by establishing norms that promote interaction and empathy between groups and encourage respect for group differences. The most important thing is to remember that we must continue to reduce the impact of racial bias and prejudice by addressing the structural and institutional conditions that perpetuate our country's history of systemic racism. While engaging in these efforts, we must also realize that addressing this issue is critical if we hope to achieve long-term goals in removing racialized barriers to belonging, opportunity and inclusivity.

REFERENCES

Adorno, T.W., Frenkel-Brunswik, E., Levinson, D.J. & Sanford, R.N. (1950). The authoritarian personality. New York: Harper and Row.

Allport, G.W. (1950). Prejudice: A problem and psychological causation. Journal of Social Issues, 4.

Allport, G.W. (1954). The nature of prejudice. Reading, MA: Addison-Wesley.

Allport, G.W. & Kramer, B.M. (1946). Some roots of prejudice. Journal of Psychology, 22, (9), 39.

Babbie, E. (1989). The practice of social research. Belmont, CA: Wadsworth Publishing Company.

Belanger, A.T. (1985). Framework for political sociology. Toronto: University of Toronto Press.

Blauner, R. (1972). Racial oppression in America. New York: Harper and Row.

Bonacich, E. (1976). Advanced capitalism and black-white relations in the United States. A split labor marker interpretation. American Sociological Review, 37, 547-559.

Brigham, J.C. (1971). Ethnic stereotypes. Psychological Bulletin, 76, 15-38.

Brigham, J.C. (1973). Ethnic stereotypes and attitudes: Different mode of analysis. Journal of Personality, 41, 206-223.

Brigham, J.C., Woodmansee, J.J. & Cook, S.W. (1976). Dimensions of verbal racial attitudes: Interracial marriage and approaches to racial equality. Journal of Social Issues, 32, (2), 9-21.

Brown, R. (1965). Social psychology. New York: The Free Press.

Calder, B.J. (1977). An attribution theory of leadership. In B.M Staw & G.R. Salancik (Eds.), New directions in organization behavior. Chicago: St. Clair Press.

Campbell, D.T. (1958). Some social psychological correlates of direction in attitude change. Social Forces, 36, 335-340.

Campbell, D.T. (1967). Stereotypes and perception of group differences. American Psychologist, 22, 817-829.

Carithers, M.W. (1970). School desegregation and racial cleavage,1954-1970: A review of the literature. The Journal of Social Issues, 26, (4), 25-48.

Cohen, L.J. (1977). The probably and the provable. Oxford: Clarendon.

Cohen, L.J. (1979). On the psychology of prediction. Whose is the fallacy? Cognition, 7, 385-407.

Collins, P. (1990). Black feminist thought: Knowledge, consciousness and the politics of empowerment. Boston: Unwin Hyman.

Cook, S.S. (1990). Toward a psychology of improving justice: Research on extending the equality principle to victims of social injustice. Journal of Social Issues, 46, (1), 147-161.

Cook, S.W. (1974). The 1954 social science statement and school desegregation. Reply to Gerard. American Psychologist, 39, 819-832.

Cook, S.W. (1978). Interpersonal and attitudinal outcomes in cooperating interracial groups. Journal of Research and Development in Education, 12, (1), 97-113.

Cook, S.W. (1987). Behavior-change implications of low involvement in an issue. Journal of Social Issues, 43, (1), 105-112.

Craig M.A & Richeson, J.A. (2018). Hispanic population growth engenders conservative shift among non-Hispanic racial minorities. Social Psychological and Personality Science, 9, (4), 383-392.

Crocker J. & Major, B. (1989). Social stigma and self-esteem. The self-protective properties of stigma. Psychological Review, 96, 608-630.

DeBose, J. (2000). The Impact of Interracial Contact on Stereotypical Perceptions. (Publication No. 9973963) Doctoral Dissertation. University of Nevada, Las Vegas.

Devine, P.G. (1989). Stereotypes and prejudice: Their automatic and controlled components. Journal of Personality and Social Psychology, 56, (1), 5-18.

Deutsch, Morton & Collins (1956). Interracial housing. In William Peterson (Ed.), American social patterns. Garden City NY: Doubleday.

Devine, P.G. & Baker, S.M. (1991). Measurement of racial stereotype sub typing. Personality and Social Psychology Bulletin, 17, (1), 44-50.

Dormhoff, G. (1990). The power elite and the state: How policy is made in America. New York: Aldine de Greyter.

Durkheim, E. (1964a). The division of labor in society. New York: The Free Press.

Durkheim, E. (1964b). The rules of sociological method. New York: The Free Press.

Eberhardt, J. (2019). Biased: Uncovering the hidden prejudice that shapes what we see, think, and do. Penguin Books

Ehrilich, H.J. (1973). The social psychology of prejudice: A systematic theoretical review and prepositional inventory of the American social psychological study of prejudice. New York: Wiley.

Einhorn, H.J. & Hogarth, R.M. (1981). Behavioral decision theory: Processes of judgment and choice. Annual Review of Psychology, 32, 53-88.

Farley, J.E. (1994). Sociology (4th ed.). Upper Saddle River, NJ: Prentice-Hall, Inc.

Farley, R. & Frey, W.H. (1964). Changes in the segregation of blacks and whites during the 1980's: Small steps toward a more integrated society. American Sociological Review, 59, 23-45.

Feagin, J.R. & Feagin, C.B. (1996). Racial and ethnic relations (5th ed.). Upper Saddle River, NJ: Prentice-Hall, Inc.

Feagin, J.R. & Sikes, M.P. (1964). Living with racism: The black middle class experience. Boston: Beacon Press.

Fiske, S.T. & Neuberg, S.I. (1990). A continuum of impression formation, from category-based to individual processes. Advances in experimental social psychology. (Vol. 23, 1-74). New York: Random House.

Funder, D.C. (1987). Errors and mistakes. Evaluating the accuracy of social judgment. Psychological Bulletin, 101, (1), 75090.

Gardner, R.C. (1973). Ethnic stereotypes: The traditional approach, a new look. The Canadian Psychologist, 14, (2), 1330148.

Gardner, R.C., Kirby, D.M. & Finlay, J.C. (1973). Ethnic stereotypes. The significance of consensus. Canadian Journal of Behavioural Science, 5, (1), 4-12.

Gordon, M.M. (1964). Assimilation in American life. New York: Oxford University Press.

Hamilton, D.L. (1981). Stereotyping and intergroup behavior: Some thoughts on the cognitive approach. In D.I. Hamilton (Ed.), Cognitive process in stereotyping and intergroup behavior. Hilldale, NJ: Erlbaum.

Hechter, M. (1975). International colonialism: The Celtic fringe in British national development. Berkeley: University of California Press.

Jussim, L. (1990). Social reality and social problems: The role of expectancies. Journal of Social Issues, 46, (2), 9-34.

Jussim, L. (1991). Social perception and social reality: A reflection-construction model. Psychological Review, 98, (1), 54-73.

Katz, D. & Braly, K. (1933). Racial stereotypes in 100 college students. Journal of Abnormal and Social Psychology, 28, 280-290.

Katz, D. & Braly, K. (1935). Racial prejudice and racial stereotypes. Journal of Abnormal Social Psychology, 30, 175-193.

Katz, D. & Braly, K. (1958). Racial stereotypes and racial prejudice. In E. Maccoby, T. M. Newcomb, & E.L. Hartley (Eds.), Readings in social psychology, (pp 40-460), New York: Holt, Rinehart and Winston.

Katz, D. & Haas, R.G. (1988). Racial ambivalence and American value conflict: Correlation and priming studies of dual cognitive structures. Journal of Personality and Social Psychology, 55, (6), 893-905.

Kendi, I. (2019). Stamped from the beginning: A definitive history of racist ideas in America (1st ed.). Oneworld Publications.

Klineberg, O. (1951). The scientific study of national stereotypes: International Social Science Bulletin, 3, 505-515.

Kluegal, J.R. (1990). Trends in whites' explanations of the black and white gap in socioeconomic status. American Sociological Review, 55, 512-525.

Kluegal, J.R. & Smith, E.R. (1986). Beliefs about inequality: Americans' view of what is and what ought to be. New York: A De Gruyter, C.

Kornblum, W. (2000). Sociology in a changing world (5th ed.). Orlando, FL: Hartcourt College Publishers.

Lippman, W. (1922). Public opinion. New York: The Free Press.

Lippman, W. (1953). Public opinion. New York: The Free Press.

Mackie, M. (1973). Arriving at "truth" by definition: The case of stereotype inaccuracy. Social Problems, 20, 431-447.

Mannheim, K. (1983). Conservatism: A contribution to the sociology of knowledge. New York: Routledge and Kegan; Paul. Rprt. 1947.

Martin, C.L. (1987). A ratio measure of sex stereotyping. Journal of Personality and Social Psychology, 52, (3), 489-499.

Marx, K. (1842). The economic and philosophic manuscripts of 1844. (D.J. Struik, Ed.), New York: International Publishers. Rpt. 1964.

McCauley, C. & Stitt, C. (1978). An individual and quantitative measure of stereotypes. Journal of Personality and Social Psychology, 36, (9), 929-940.

McCauley, C., Stitt, C. & Segal, M. (1980). Stereotyping: From prejudice to prediction. Psychological Bulletin, 87, (1), 195-208.

Merton, R. (1948). Discrimination and the American creed. In R.M. MacIver (Ed.), Discrimination and national welfare. New York: Institute for Religious and Social Studies, Harper.

National Opinion Research Center (NORC) (1991). Annual general social survey, cumulative codebook. Chicago: University of Chicago Press.

Noel, D.L. (1968). A theory of the origin of ethnic stratification. Social Problems, 16, 157-172.

O'Brien, J. (2016). The production of reality: Essays and readings on social Interaction. Sage publication Inc. 373.

Olzak, S. & Izak, S. (1992). The dynamic of ethnic competition and conflict, Stanford, CA: Stanford University Press.

Park, R.E. (1924). The concept of social distance. Journal of Applied Sociology, 8, 339-344.

Parsons, T. (Ed). (1969). American sociology perspectives, problems, methods. New York: Basic Books.

Pettigrew, T.F. (1964). New patterns of racism: The different worlds of 1984 and 1964. Rutgers Law Review, 1, 673-706.

Rothbart, M. & Joh, O.P. (1985). Social categorization and behavioral episodes: A cognitive analysis of the affects of intergroup contact. Journal of Social Issues, 41, (3), 91-104.

St. John, N. (1963). De facto segregation and interracial association in high school. <u>Sociology of Education</u>, <u>37,</u> (4), 326-344.

Schuman, H. & Steele, C. (1986). Racial attitudes in America: Trends and interpretations. <u>Public Opinion Quarterly</u>, <u>50,</u> (4), 584.

Simpson, E.G. & Yinger, J.M. (1965). <u>Racial and cultural minorities</u>, New York: Harper and Row.

Smith, E.R. & Zárate, M.A. (1992). Exemplar-based model of social judgment. <u>Psychological Review</u>, <u>99,</u> (1), 3-21.

Spears, R., Oakes, P., Ellemers, N. & Hasham, A.S. (1997). <u>The social psychology of stereotyping and group life</u>. Cambridge, MA.: Blackwell Publishers Ltd.

St. John, N. (1963). Defacto segregation and interracial association in high school. <u>Sociology of Education</u>, <u>37,</u> 326-344.

Stanger, C. & Schaller, M. (1996). Stereotypes as individual and collective representations. C.N. Macrae, C. Stangor & M. Hewstone (Eds.), <u>Stereotypes and stereotyping</u> (pp. 3-40). New York: Guilford Press.

Starr, D. (2020). Meet the psychologist exploring unconscious bias - and its tragic consequences for society. <u>https://www.sciencemag.org/news/2020/03/</u>

meet-psychologist-exploring-unconscious-bias-and-its-tragic-consequences-society

Stouffer, S.A. (1949). The American soldier: Adjustment during army life. Princeton, NJ: Princeton University Press, Vol. 1, p. 506.

Taft, R. (1959). Ethnic stereotypes, attitudes, and familiarity: Australia. Journal of Social Psychology, 49, 177-186.

Taylor, S.E. (1981). A categorization approach to stereotyping. In D.L. Hamilton (Ed.), Cognitive processes in stereotyping and intergroup behavior, (pp. 83-107). Hillsdale, NJ: Lawrence Erlbaum Associates, Inc.

U.S. Bureau of the Census (1996). World population profile.

Vinacke, E.W. (1957). Stereotypes as social concepts. The Journal of Social Psychology, 46, 229-243.

Weigel, R.H. & Howes, P.W. (1985). Conceptions of racial prejudice: Symbolic racism reconsidered. Journal of Social Issues, 41, (3), 117-138.

Wilner, D. (1955). Human relations in interracial housing: A study of the contact hypothesis. Minneapolis, MN: University of Minnesota Press.